Foundation

THIS BOOK WAS DONATED BY
The Sacramento Public Library Foundation
Books and Materials Endowment

The Sacramento Public Library gratefully acknowledges this
contribution to support and improve Library services in the community.

sac
lib SACRAMENTO PUBLIC LIBRARY

American ANIMALS

MOUNTAIN GOATS

Meryl Magby

PowerKiDS
press

New York

For my friend Maud Deitch, who loves the Mountain Goats

Published in 2014 by The Rosen Publishing Group, Inc.
29 East 21st Street, New York, NY 10010

First Edition

Editor: Amelie von Zumbusch
Book Design: Ashley Drago
Layout Design: Colleen Bialecki

Photo Credits: Cover Craig K. Lorenz/Photo Researchers/Getty Images; p. 4 Diane Garcia/Shutterstock.com; p. 5 Stokkete/Shutterstock.com; p. 7 Paul E. Tessier/Photodisc/Getty Images; p. 8 Tom Reichner/Shutterstock.com; p. 9 Mark Newman/Lonely Planet Images/Getty Images; p. 10 Jyeshern Cheng/E+/Getty Images; p. 11 Ken Gillespie/All Canada Photos/Getty Images; pp. 12–13 Noah Clayton/Getty Images; p. 14 Julie Lubick/Shutterstock.com; p. 15 Nina B/Shutterstock.com; p. 16 Henryk Sadura/Shutterstock.com; p. 17 Joel Sartore/National Geographic/Getty Images; p. 18 Mark Newman/Lonely Planet Images/Getty Images; p. 19 Paul McCormick/Stockbyte/Getty Images; p. 10 yykkaa/Shutterstock.com; p. 21 Scenic Shutterbug/Shutterstock.com; p. 22 Blue Iris/Shutterstock.com.

Library of Congress Cataloging-in-Publication Data

Magby, Meryl.
  Mountain goats / by Meryl Magby. — 1st ed.
      p. cm. — (American animals)
  Includes index.
  ISBN 978-1-4777-0790-6 (library binding) — ISBN 978-1-4777-0952-8 (pbk.) — ISBN 978-1-4777-0953-5 (6-pack)
  1. Mountain goat—Juvenile literature. I. Title. II. Series: Magby, Meryl. American animals.
  QL737.U53M22373 2014
  599.64'75—dc23

2012049463

Manufactured in the United States of America

CPSIA Compliance Information: Batch #S13PK6: For Further Information contact Rosen Publishing, New York, New York at 1-800-237-9932

Contents

Amazing Climbers

Mountain goats are also sometimes known as Rocky Mountain goats.

Mountain goats are native to northwestern North America. These amazing animals have **adapted** to live high in the mountains. Very few animals or plants can survive in a mountain goat's **habitat**! Mountain goats can climb steep mountain cliffs and walk narrow ledges. Their special hooves help keep them from slipping. Few animal **predators** can chase them up the rocky mountainside. Their thick, furry coats keep them warm in even the coldest, windiest weather.

Though they are called goats, mountain goats are not true goats. Rather, they are goat antelopes. However, they are related to true goats, sheep, chamois, and musk oxen.

Unlike mountain goats, the goats found on farms are true goats. Both mountain goats and true goats are great climbers, though.

High Mountain Homes

Mountain goats live among the high mountain ranges of the northwestern United States and western Canada. These include the Coast Mountains, Cascade Mountains, and Rocky Mountains. Their **native range** reaches from Alaska in the northwest to Idaho in the southeast.

People have also introduced mountain goats to places outside of their native range, such as Utah, South Dakota, and Colorado.

A few mountain goats live in forests near the Pacific Ocean. However, most make their homes high in the mountains. They live on rocky cliffs that are between 5,000 and 13,000 feet (1,524–3,962 m) high. This is so high that trees rarely grow there! In winter, mountain goat habitats get very snowy, icy, and windy. Mountain goats spend their summers in green mountain **meadows**.

Hooves and Horns

Mountain goats have double coats of white hair to keep them warm and dry. Each coat has an inner layer of thick, short hair and an outer layer of longer hair. Their white coats help mountain goats blend in with their snowy habitats. Mountain goats also have shiny, dark horns that curve backward.

An adult mountain goat's horns are usually between 8 and 10 inches (20–25 cm) long.

Each of a mountain goat's four hooves has two toes. Mountain goat toes can spread wide to give the animals amazing **balance** as they climb. The bottom of each toe is covered by a rough pad. These pads help mountain goats grip steep rocks and slippery ice.

Although they have thick coats, mountain goats have never been tamed and raised for their wool.

Not Picky Eaters

Mountain goats are **herbivores**. This means they eat only plants. However, they are not very picky eaters. This is because so few plants grow in their high mountain habitats. They have to eat what they can find. Mountain goats eat grasses, mosses, shrubs, and other plants depending on the time of year.

Mountain goats will eat flowers. Any plants can seem appetizing when food is hard to come by.

In the summer, mountain goats eat grass and other plants in high mountain meadows. In the winter, it can be hard to find plants under the snow and ice. Then, mountain goats look for lichen, hemlock, and shrubs. Mountain goats also stay healthy by licking salt **deposits**.

Mountain goats love salt. This one is licking salt from a road. Mountain goats have even been known to lick hikers' sweaty gear in order to get salt!

Mountain Goat Facts

1. Mountain goats often weigh between 100 and 300 pounds (45–136 kg). Males are generally heavier than females.

2. Mountain goat horns do not fall off, as deer antlers do. Instead, they get longer and thicker each year. You can tell how old a mountain goat is by how many rings its horns have.

3. Mountain goats can survive in temperatures as low as -50° F (-46° C). They can also stand winds that blow at speeds of 100 miles per hour (161 km/h)!

4. Mountain goats are amazing jumpers. They can jump nearly 12 feet (4 m) in one jump! They often jump from one rocky cliff to another.

5. Sometimes people confuse mountain goats with Dall sheep. Dall sheep also live in mountain habitats in northwestern North America. They also have horns and white coats.

6. Mountain goats are the largest mammals to live as high up in the mountains as they do.

7. Scientists think that there are between 40,000 and 100,000 mountain goats in North America today.

Summer and Winter

Mountain goats spend the summer months in high mountain meadows. There, they graze for food in the morning and at night in small groups, called bands. In the afternoon, they rest. Males stay separate from female goats and their babies. Mountain goats shed their long outer coats in the summer. They rub their bodies against rocks and trees to help pull the hair off.

The summer is more relaxing for mountain goats since they have much more vegetation to eat.

When winter comes, mountain goats form much larger bands. These bands move further down the mountainside, where it does not get as cold and snowy. The goats spend more time looking for food and less time resting during the winter.

The process of shedding, shown here, is also called molting.

Fighting Each Other

Mountain goats are **aggressive**. This means they often start fights with each other. Female goats, called nannies, fight with other nannies. Their fights are about which nannies get the best spots for eating and resting.

A mountain goat's horns can be very dangerous, but most of their fights are fairly harmless.

Male goats, called billies, also fight with each other. Their fights happen each fall, during mountain goats' **mating** season. They fight to decide which billies will mate with nearby nannies.

Mountain goats fight with their sharp horns. However, they do not butt their heads together, as most animals with horns or antlers do. Instead, they aim their horns at the other goats' sides or backs.

Mountain goats are noisier during the mating season. Billies lick nannies' coats and kick at their legs during this period, too.

Mountain Goat Kids

Baby mountain goats are born each year in late spring or early summer. They are called kids. Kids tend to weigh between 5 and 8 pounds (2–4 kg) at birth. They can stand up almost right away! After about a week, they can follow their mothers up steep cliffs, too.

Many nannies have just one kid at a time, though a few have twins.

Nannies are very protective of their kids. They lead them out of danger and defend them against predators.

Kids drink only their mothers' milk at first so that they can grow bigger and stronger. After about four months, they start eating plants instead. A kid stays with its mother until she has another baby the next year. Mountain goats can live to be about 12 years old in the wild.

Predators and Hunting

Few predators can catch a mountain goat high in the mountains. Mountain lions are the only predators that can chase mountain goats up rocky slopes. Eagles sometimes swoop in from above to grab kids, though. Brown bears, lynx, and gray wolves can catch mountain goats only when they leave the mountains for forests or valleys.

Golden eagles use their speed, excellent eyesight, and powerful claws to snatch a variety of prey.

People also hunt mountain goats. For many years, native peoples in the northwest have made blankets out of mountain goat fur. They also use mountain goat **hides** for the soles of their shoes. Today, people can hunt mountain goats in several states in the western United States and in parts of Canada.

Learning More

Mountain goats are not in danger of dying out. Only small numbers of mountain goats can be hunted each year in the United States and Canada. This keeps their **population** from getting too small. Many mountain goats live in national parks and wildlife **refuges**. There, their habitats are kept safe as well.

Scientists still want to learn more about mountain goats. Mountain goats are hard to study because they live so high in the mountains! In the future, we may know even more about these amazing animals.

Living at altitudes of 14,000 feet (4,267 m) or more makes mountain goats hard to study.

Glossary

adapted (uh-DAP-ted) Changed to fit requirements.

aggressive (uh-GREH-siv) Ready to fight.

balance (BAL-ens) Staying steady.

deposits (dih-PAH-zutz) Things that are left behind.

habitat (HA-buh-tat) The kind of land where an animal or a plant naturally lives.

herbivores (ER-buh-vorz) Animals that eat only plants.

hides (HYDS) The skins of animals.

mating (MAYT-ing) Coming together to make babies.

meadows (MEH-dohz) Areas of grassland.

native range (NAY-tiv RAYNJ) The places in which an animal naturally lived, before people introduced it to new areas.

population (pop-yoo-LAY-shun) A group of animals or people living in the same place.

predators (PREH-duh-terz) Animals that kill other animals for food.

refuges (REH-fyoo-jez) Places where something is kept safe.

Index

Websites

Due to the changing nature of Internet links, PowerKids Press has developed an online list of websites related to the subject of this book. This site is updated regularly. Please use this link to access the list:

www.powerkidslinks.com/amer/goat/